D1327433

Mapping Earth from Space

Robert Snedden

Chicago, Illinois

www.heinemannraintree.com
Visit our website to find out more information about Heinemann-Raintree books.

To order:
☎ Phone 888-454-2279
▨ Visit www.heinemannraintree.com to browse our catalog and order online.

Edited by Adam Miller, Andrew Farrow, and Adrian Vigliano
Designed by Philippa Jenkins
Original illustrations © Capstone Global Library Ltd.
Illustrated by KJA-artists.com
Picture research by Tracy Cummins
Production by Alison Parsons
Originated by Dot Gradations
Printed and bound in China by South China Printing Company Ltd

14 13 12 11 10
10 9 8 7 6 5 4 3 2 1

Library of Congress Cataloging-in-Publication Data
Snedden, Robert.
  Mapping Earth from Space / Robert Snedden.
    p. cm. — (Science Missions)
  Includes bibliographical references and index.
  ISBN 978-1-4109-3826-8 (hc)
1. Earth sciences—Remote sensing—Juvenile literature. 2. Earth—Remote-sensing images—Juvenile literature. I. Title.
  QE33.2.R4S64 2011
  526.9'82—dc22

2009053333

Acknowledgments
The author and publishers are grateful to the following for permission to reproduce copyright material: Amazon Conservation Team **p.46**; Corbis/© MAPS.com **p.7 top**; ESA/CNES/ ARIANESPACE-S.Corvaja **p.12**; ESA/AOES Medialab **p.39**; Getty Images/Ian Logan **p.45**; NASA **pp.4&5**; NASA/GSFC/MITI/ERSDAC/ JAROS, and U.S./Japan ASTER Science Team **p.7 bottom**; NASA/Jesse Allen/ Goddard Land Processes data archives **pp.8&9**; NASA **p.10**; NASA/GSFC/LaRC/JPL, MISR Team **p.15**; NASA/Barbara Summey, NASA GSFC **p.16**; NASA/GSFC/METI/ERSDAC/ JAROS, and U.S./ Japan ASTER Science Team **p.17**; NASA/Jesse Allen, NASA Earth Observatory **p.18**; NASA/Jeff Schmaltz, MODIS Rapid Response Team **p.19**; NASA/Courtesy of Orbital Sciences Corporation **p.21**; NASA/Goddard Space Flight Center (NASA-GSFC) **pp.22&23**; NASA/Landsat **p.24**; NASA/Landsat **p.24**; NASA/JSC **pp.26&27**; NASA/Goddard Space Flight Center **p.28**; NASA **p.29**; NASA **p.30**; NASA/Jesse Allen/Earth Observatory/Goddard Earth Sciences DAAC **p.31**; NASA/MODIS Land Group, Goddard Space Flight Center **pp.32&33**; NASA/Goddard Space Flight Center, The SeaWiFS Project/GeoEye **p.36**; NASA/JPL **p.37**; NASA **p.38**; NASA/Marc Imhoff/ GSFC/Christopher Elvidge of NOAA NGDC/ Mayhew and Robert Simmon, NASA GSFC **pp.42&43**; NASA/MODIS Rapid Response Team at Goddard Space Flight Center **p.47**; NASA **p.48**; NASA/Raytheon **p.49**; National Geographic Stock/PAUL NICKLEN **p.35**; Naval Research Laboratory **p.41**; NOAA **p.40**; R. Scott Zoller-Gritz **p.11**; shutterstock/Vladislav Gurfinkel **pp.50&51**.

Cover photograph of Central Asia's Uvs Nuur Basin reproduced with the permission of NASA/ GSFC/METI/ERSDAC/JAROS, and U.S./Japan ASTER Science Team.

We would like to thank Geza Gyuk for his invaluable help in the preparation of this book.

Every effort has been made to contact copyright holders of any material reproduced in this book. Any omissions will be rectified in subsequent printings if notice is given to the publisher.

Disclaimer
All the Internet addresses (URLs) given in this book were valid at the time of going to press. However, due to the dynamic nature of the Internet, some addresses may have changed, or sites may have changed or ceased to exist since publication. While the author and publisher regret any inconvenience this may cause readers, no responsibility for any such changes can be accepted by either the author or the publisher.

CONTENTS

Some words are printed in bold, **like this**. You can find out what they mean by looking in the glossary. You can also look out for them in the **WORD STORE** box at the bottom of each page.

The space shuttle Endeavor deploys a special antenna as part of a mission for mapping Earth. The antenna is now part of a device that takes 3D images of Earth's surface.

GOING FURTHER TO
SEE BETTER

In 2009 a stone tablet was found in a cave in Spain. Scratched on it is a map of the area around the cave. It shows features such as a river, a mountain, and good places to hunt deer. The remarkable thing about this map is that it was made 14,000 years ago. It is a snapshot in time from long ago.

A map can show you the street where you live, or it can show you the whole world. A map lets you see the features of the landscape. It shows you how the land changes between one place and another and how that land is used.

Today, a fleet of **satellites** is **orbiting**, or circling around, Earth. These satellites point their **sensors** (detectors) and cameras toward us. The information they send is used to produce ever-changing maps of our planet and its resources. Among them are the satellites of the Earth Observing System run by the National Aeronautics and Space Administration (NASA). Their mission is to provide information about Earth's land, sea, air, and life.

Seeing Earth from space is helping scientists to understand our world better than ever before.

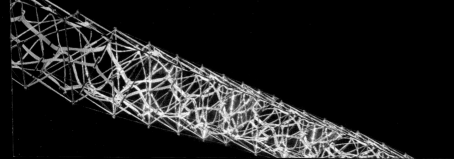

Mapmaking

People have always wanted to make maps of the places they live. It is good to know where you are in the world, and which direction to set out in if you want to get to somewhere else.

In the past, people could only make maps of places they or someone they knew had actually visited. A mapmaking expedition was a journey of exploration and discovery.

What is a map?

A map is like a picture of all or part of Earth's surface. It would be impossible, and confusing, to show every single feature, so a map will show things that the mapmaker thinks will be useful. Different maps can be made for different purposes. For example, a map for car drivers will concentrate on roads, intersections, and place-names, while a map for hikers will show paths, streams, forests, and mountains.

To understand and use a map, you need to know what you are looking at. You need to know what part of Earth it shows. For example, a map of Chicago would not be very useful if you were planning a trip to Paris. You also need to know how to figure out direction on the map. For this reason, most maps have north at the top. You also need to know how the different features, such as rivers, roads, airports, and so on, are shown. Maps have a key, called a **legend**, that explains the meaning of the symbols used on the map.

Mapping from space

Images from satellites can be straightforward photographs of the surface of Earth, just like photos you could take yourself if you went up there with a camera. But, just like a map, they can also be used to highlight different features of interest.

As we will see, satellites can look at Earth in ways that are beyond the range of human senses. The instruments on a satellite can pick out things like differences in temperature and the amounts of pollution in the atmosphere. They can show where plants grow and help track the movements of wildlife. All of these things can be mapped.

WORD STORE   **legend** list that explains the different symbols used on a map

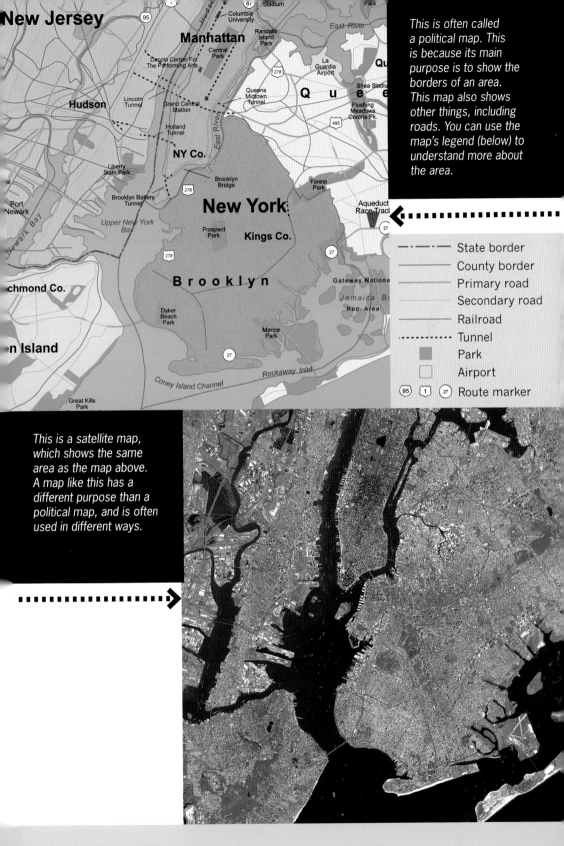

New Jersey

95

Manhattan

Columbia University

Stadium

Randalls Island Park

East River

Park

Lincoln Center For The Performing Arts

Central Park

La Guardia Airport

278

Qu

Hudson

Lincoln Tunnel

Grand Central Station

Queens Midtown Tunnel

Q u e e

Shea Stadium

Holland Tunnel

Flushing Meadows Corona Pk.

495

NY Co.

Liberty State Park

Brooklyn Bridge

Forest Park

Port Newark

Brooklyn Battery Tunnel

278

New York

Aqueduct Race Track

27

Newark Bay

Upper New York Bay

Prospect Park

Kings Co.

27

278

chmond Co.

B r o o k l y n

Gateway National

Jamaica B

Rec. Area

Dyker Beach Park

Marine Park

n Island

27

Coney Island Channel

Rockaway Inlet

Great Kills Park

This is often called a political map. This is because its main purpose is to show the borders of an area. This map also shows other things, including roads. You can use the map's legend (below) to understand more about the area.

◀ ▪▪▪▪▪▪▪▪▪▪▪▪▪▪▪▪▪▪

─ ▪ ─ ▪ ─ ▪ ─	State border
───────	County border
───────	Primary road
───────	Secondary road
───────	Railroad
▪▪▪▪▪▪▪▪▪	Tunnel
■	Park
▢	Airport
95 1 27	Route marker

This is a satellite map, which shows the same area as the map above. A map like this has a different purpose than a political map, and is often used in different ways.

▪▪▪▪▪▪▪▪▪▪▪▪▪▪▪▪▪ ➤

7

EARTH
OBSERVATORIES

On April 12, 1961, Russian cosmonaut (astronaut) Yuri Gagarin radioed ground control, saying, "The Earth is blue. How wonderful. It is amazing." He was the first human to see Earth from space with his own eyes. But it was not the first time we had seen Earth from far away. **Satellites** got there first.

The first picture of our planet sent back from space was a fuzzy black-and-white image taken by the satellite Explorer 6 on August 14, 1959. It is hard to see that what the image shows is a planet at all, but it is easy to imagine the excitement of seeing the very first picture of planet Earth. On April 1, 1960, the Tiros-1 weather satellite beamed down the first television pictures of Earth from **orbit**. Since then we have never stopped watching our world.

Fifty years later, we are still fascinated, still wanting to know more about our planet. Dozens of Earth-observation satellites keep continual, detailed watch over Earth. They let us see the consequences of our actions today, and they help us plan for the future.

This NASA satellite image shows the islands of northeast Canada, which are located near Greenland.

Landsat satellites

The modern period of Earth satellite observations began with the launch of the Landsat satellites in the 1970s. This important project was a joint venture between NASA and the U.S. Geological Survey (USGS). For nearly 40 years, the Landsat satellites have returned detailed photographs of Earth's landmasses, allowing us to keep track of the changes brought about by people and nature. We have learned a lot from Landsat—not only about Earth, but also about how to improve the instruments we use for watching it.

Earth Observing System

Today, some of our most important "eyes on the world" are the satellites of the Earth Observing System (EOS). EOS is one of NASA's most important programs for long-term observations of Earth's land and oceans, its atmosphere, and the living things that make their home there. The EOS satellites are the responsibility of the Earth Science Projects Division, operating out of the Goddard Space Flight Center in Maryland.

Planning for the EOS mission began in the 1980s and took shape throughout the 1990s. The goal is to develop a scientific understanding of Earth and how it responds to changes.

An artist's impression of the Landsat 7 satellite.

These changes can be natural, such as erupting volcanoes. They can also be caused by humans, such as the effects of our car exhaust on the atmosphere. By mapping the changes taking place on Earth, NASA scientist Dr. Ghassem Asrar described the goal of EOS as enabling "improved prediction of climate, weather, and natural hazards for present and future generations."

Landsat 7 was the last of the Landsat satellites to be launched, heading into orbit on April 15, 1999. It is now included as part of the EOS mission and continues to send back images of Earth.

WORKING WITH LANDSAT 7

Landsat 7 was the latest of the Landsat satellites to be launched, heading into orbit on April 15, 1999. It is considered part of the EOS mission and continues to send back images of the Earth. Including Landsat in EOS pleased senior project engineer Terry Arvidson (pictured below), who joined the Landsat program in 1979. After a recent decision by the USGS, Landsat data can be given away for free, rather than sold. This is good news for scientists, who can now work with the large numbers of images necessary for global change studies, without worrying about how to pay for the data.

Terry enjoys working with others toward a common goal. She said, "I can talk science to the science folks, spacecraft to the spacecraft folks, operations to the operations folks, and help one group understand the other's requirements." She's made friends around the world, working with engineers in other countries that receive Landsat data at their own ground stations. And she also likes "knowing that I'm working on a project that benefits mankind, that's going to help us understand what we're doing to planet Earth and how we need to change in order to preserve the Earth for future generations."

Into orbit

Before we go on to meet some of the star performers of the EOS, let's take a look at how a satellite actually gets into orbit.

Most satellites are launched into orbit inside the nose cone of a rocket **launcher**. The launcher is the vehicle that carries a satellite into orbit. The heavier the satellite, the more powerful the launcher will need to be to lift it into space.

Another method used has been to carry the satellite in the **payload bay**, or cargo hold, of the space shuttle. When the shuttle reaches orbit, the satellite is released and nudged into position with small rockets. Later, we will see a satellite that was fired into orbit from an aircraft.

Types of orbit

Satellites can be placed into different orbits around Earth, depending on what scientists want to do with them.

Equatorial orbit

An equatorial orbit is the sort of orbit followed by spacecraft with astronauts aboard. They travel in a route around Earth's equator. The International Space Station is in an equatorial orbit.

Polar orbit

A polar orbit is an orbit that goes north to south around Earth, passing over the North and South Poles. As Earth spins beneath the satellite, the satellite can monitor the planet's whole surface.

This rocket is being prepared to launch a new satellite into orbit.

WORD STORE   **launcher** vehicle that carries a satellite up into orbit

HOW FAST?

How fast a satellite travels around Earth—what is called its orbital velocity—depends on how far above the surface it is. A space shuttle, in orbit 300 kilometers (186 miles) above Earth, travels at roughly 28,000 km/h (17,400 mph). Communications satellites in geostationary orbits 35,790 kilometers (22,240 miles) above Earth have an orbital speed of around 11,000 kilometers (7,000 miles) per hour.

Geostationary orbit

A geostationary orbit is an orbit in which the satellite travels around Earth at the same speed the planet turns. As a result, the satellite appears suspended over a single point on Earth's surface. Communications satellites are often placed in geostationary orbits.

Sun-synchronous orbit

A sun-synchronous orbit is an orbit that is partway between a polar and equatorial orbit, tilted so that the satellite passes the equator at the same local time on every orbit. The sun-synchronous orbit also moves a little to the east each day, to keep pace with Earth's orbit around the Sun.

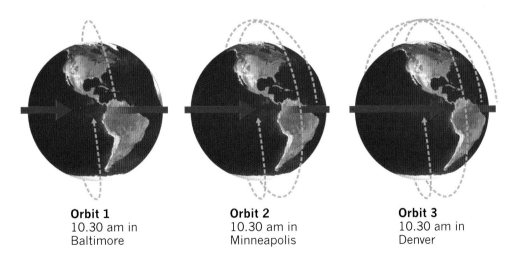

Orbit 1
10.30 am in Baltimore

Orbit 2
10.30 am in Minneapolis

Orbit 3
10.30 am in Denver

This example of a sun-synchronous orbit shows a satellite (the dotted line) passing over three cities that are in three different time zones. This kind of orbit lets the satellite pass over each city at the same local time in each time zone.

WORD STORE   **payload bay** the space shuttle's cargo hold

Terra

Terra is an international mission put together jointly by the United States, Canada, and Japan. It is the flagship (most important) satellite of the EOS and was the first of the EOS satellites to be launched. Since 2000 Terra has been engaged in a 15-year data-gathering mission. This mission will help researchers build up a detailed picture of the impact of human activities on our world.

Terra was launched into orbit on December 18, 1999, and follows a sun-synchronous orbit 705 kilometers (438 miles) above Earth. This means that its view of Earth's surface is always lit by the Sun in the same way.

WHAT'S IN A NAME?

Terra's original name was EOS AM-1. In 1998 NASA held a competition to find something better to call it. Over 1,000 students from grades 8 to 12 from all over the world took part. The winner was Sasha Jones, a student from St. Louis. Sasha chose the name Terra because it means "Earth."

Terra's science goals

Terra has several goals:

1. It aims to measure changes in Earth across the seasons by monitoring snow and ice cover, surface temperature changes, and cloud cover.

2. It aims to monitor long-term changes in the climate and the **environment**. The environment includes the world's living things and the places they make their homes.

3. It aims to improve our ability to detect the effect of human activity on Earth, such as **climate change**. Climate change refers to changes in Earth's climate that many scientists believe are caused by human activity.

4. It aims to help in developing better ways of predicting natural disasters, such as floods and volcanic eruptions.

WORD STORE   **climate change** changes in the Earth's climate that many scientists believe are a result of human activities

This image was taken by MISR (see page 17) aboard Terra. It shows huge fires raging near Los Angeles in 2009.

Through the window

A satellite that is being placed into a precise orbit has to be launched at a particular time. This is called the launch window. Terra had to be launched between 10:30 and 11:00 a.m. Pacific Standard Time (the standard Pacific time zone).

As launch time approached, mission managers grew worried that high winds would blow the Atlas rocket off course. Just before time ran out, the rocket engineers gave the go-ahead for launch. With 10 seconds to spare, the rocket lifted off the pad to begin its ascent into space. Terra project manager Kevin Grady said, "It all begins with a launch support team that is resourceful and adept [skilled] at identifying and solving problems quickly. But to launch a successful mission of this scope, you also need a robust spacecraft and a well-prepared flight operations team. Fortunately for Terra, we had both."

Terra's instruments

The Terra spacecraft, or "bus," was designed at NASA's Goddard Space Flight Center, and assembled and tested by the Lockheed Martin company. On board it carries five high-tech instrument packages and weighs a total of 4,645 kilograms (10,506 pounds).

The first instrument package, the Advanced Spaceborne Thermal Emission and Reflection Radiometer (ASTER), was built jointly by the United States and Japan. It is being used to make detailed maps of temperature differences across Earth's surface and of the way in which different surfaces reflect light. It can also produce detailed three-dimensional images of surface features. ASTER provides information on a range of Earth features, such as plant cover, volcanic eruptions, and changes in land use.

The Clouds and the Earth Radiant Energy System (CERES) was developed at the Langley Research Center, in Virginia. It measures Earth's **energy balance**. This is the balance between the energy that comes in to Earth from the Sun and the energy that is reflected back into space from land, sea, and clouds. It is the Sun's energy that powers Earth's weather systems. Among other things, CERES is examining the effects of cloud cover on climate, as well as the impact of major events such as floods and volcanic eruptions.

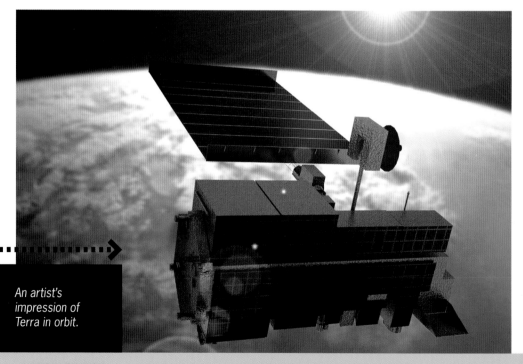

An artist's impression of Terra in orbit.

WORD STORE   **energy balance** balance between energy that comes to Earth from the Sun and energy that is reflected back to space

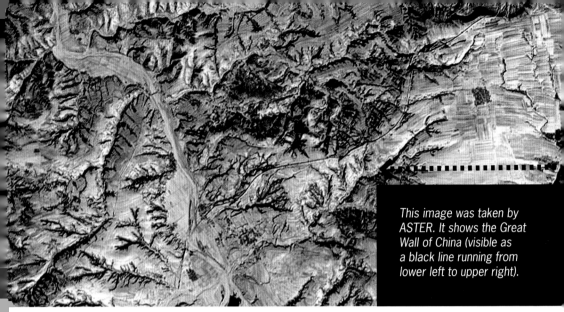

This image was taken by ASTER. It shows the Great Wall of China (visible as a black line running from lower left to upper right).

The Multi-Angle Imaging SpectroRadiometer (MISR) was developed at the Jet Propulsion Laboratory, in California. It is unlike any other space-based device. Most satellite instruments either point straight down to Earth or look across it, but MISR views Earth from a group of cameras pointing in nine different directions. As Terra passes overhead, the MISR cameras photograph each part of the surface from different angles. These images let researchers see how the Sun's light reflects back into space from Earth, and how this is affected by particles (tiny pieces of matter) in the atmosphere, such as those caused by pollution.

The Moderate Resolution Imaging Spectroradiometer (MODIS) was developed at Goddard. It has a very wide field-of-view camera. In a single orbit it can capture an image of half the continental United States. It can keep track of levels of carbon dioxide in the atmosphere and detect fires, even through thick smoke. The USDA Forest Service uses MODIS to spot forest fires and respond to them rapidly.

MODIS also monitors sea temperature changes and concentrations of **phytoplankton** in the oceans. These tiny organisms are at the beginning of the ocean food chain. This means they are the first step in the way food energy transfers between living things in the ocean, from smallest to largest. So, phytoplankton are very important to the health of the oceans.

Measurement of Pollution in the Troposphere (MOPITT) was built by the Canadian Space Agency. The troposphere is the part of Earth's atmosphere that we live in, from the surface to about 20 kilometers (12 miles) above. MOPITT measures levels of carbon monoxide gas and the way in which it moves through the lower atmosphere.

WORD STORE   **phytoplankton** microscopic organisms that live in water and can make their own food from the Sun's energy

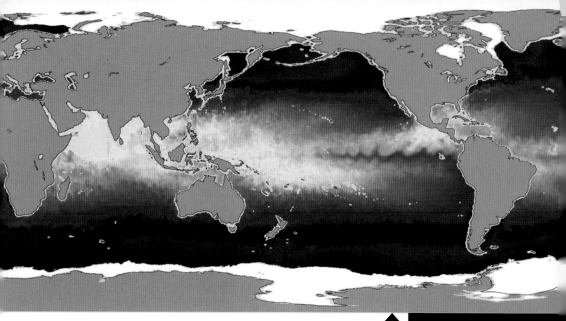

Aqua

Aqua, which lifted off from Vandenberg Air Force Base on May 4, 2002, is in many ways Terra's twin. It shares some of the same scientific instruments. While *terra* means "Earth," *aqua* means "water." Its mission is to gather information on Earth's water cycle, the movement of water between the oceans, the atmosphere, and the land. It measures evaporation of water from the oceans, rainfall, and snow and ice cover.

This Aqua image shows the ocean surface temperatures of the entire world. The lowest temperatures are shown as dark green, and the highest are yellow.

Like Terra, Aqua was launched into a sun-synchronous orbit. Terra's orbit around Earth is timed so that it passes from north to south across the equator in the morning, while Aqua passes south to north over the equator in the afternoon. This lets the researchers compare conditions in an area at different times of the day. As Aqua began its first year of observations, *Popular Science* magazine gave it a "Best of What's New" award.

The A-Train

Aqua was the first of a series of Earth-observing satellites flying in formation around the world. Together they make up the Afternoon constellation of satellites, or the A-Train. By 2010, the A-Train consisted of five satellites: Aqua, CloudSat, CALIPSO, PARASOL, and Aura.

CloudSat's primary role is in hurricane research. It carries an advanced **radar** system that shows how clouds are structured and can give a side-on view of a hurricane.

WORD STORE   **ozone** high-atmosphere oxygen that filters harmful radiation
radar instrument that determines the distance to an object

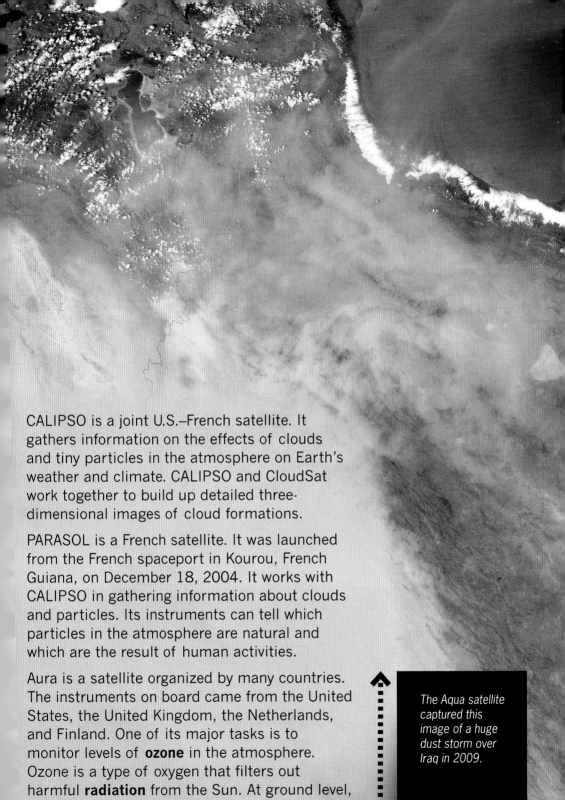

CALIPSO is a joint U.S.–French satellite. It gathers information on the effects of clouds and tiny particles in the atmosphere on Earth's weather and climate. CALIPSO and CloudSat work together to build up detailed three-dimensional images of cloud formations.

PARASOL is a French satellite. It was launched from the French spaceport in Kourou, French Guiana, on December 18, 2004. It works with CALIPSO in gathering information about clouds and particles. Its instruments can tell which particles in the atmosphere are natural and which are the result of human activities.

Aura is a satellite organized by many countries. The instruments on board came from the United States, the United Kingdom, the Netherlands, and Finland. One of its major tasks is to monitor levels of **ozone** in the atmosphere. Ozone is a type of oxygen that filters out harmful **radiation** from the Sun. At ground level, though, ozone is harmful.

The Aqua satellite captured this image of a huge dust storm over Iraq in 2009.

WORD STORE   **radiation** energy in the form of waves

OCO: A lost satellite

Space research is complicated, and things do not always go according to plan. Aqua was not intended to be the lead satellite in the A-Train. The Orbiting Carbon Observatory (OCO) should have taken that position. Unfortunately, it did not make it into orbit.

At 1:55 a.m. on February 24, 2009, a Taurus XL launcher lifted off from the launchpad at Vandenberg Air Force Base. At the top of the rocket was the OCO. "The mission is off to a great start!" said NASA spokesman Steve Cole, who witnessed the launch.

For the first part of the flight, a **payload** fairing protects the satellite. A fairing is like a shell that encloses the satellite and prevents it from being damaged as the rocket accelerates through the atmosphere. As soon as the rocket is high enough, the fairing is disposed of.

The fairing around the OCO should have released a few seconds after the second-stage booster rocket ignited. But it did not. This meant that when the third-stage booster lit, it now had the additional weight of the fairing to cope with, as well as the OCO. The stage-three rockets were not powerful enough for the task. The OCO did not reach the velocity it needed to make it into orbit. Instead, it curved back toward Earth, fortunately crashing harmlessly into the ocean near Antarctica.

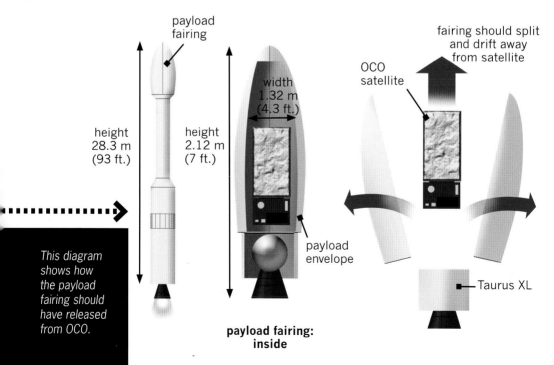

payload fairing

height 28.3 m (93 ft.)

width 1.32 m (4.3 ft.)

height 2.12 m (7 ft.)

payload envelope

This diagram shows how the payload fairing should have released from OCO.

payload fairing: inside

fairing should split and drift away from satellite

OCO satellite

Taurus XL

A big loss

"Everybody was really hanging their heads," said Steve Cole in an interview. "It's a big loss. People were really . . . looking forward to this. We'll pick ourselves up and keep on moving. We're not stopping the global warming and carbon dioxide research because of this."

NASA gave the go-ahead for OCO in 2002. The cost of the mission was over $200 million. That is a lot of time and money to see sink without a trace in the Antarctic Ocean. The OCO team want to be given the chance to try again, but that will depend on getting funding for a second shot.

What might have been

If OCO had made it into orbit, it would have given scientists hugely detailed information on levels of carbon dioxide in the atmosphere. It would have greatly increased our understanding of how this **greenhouse gas** is released into the atmosphere, and also how it is taken up by oceans and forests.

OCO launching in 2009.

IMAGE PROCESSING

Most **satellites** are not taking photographs of Earth that we can look at directly. Satellite data-gathering instruments can capture images in wavelengths of light like **infrared** and **ultraviolet** light that are invisible to our senses. Other instruments use **radar** to map the surface of Earth.

Each of these different forms of data gathering can be used to highlight various things in the atmosphere or on the surface of Earth that the researchers are interested in.

The information gathered by the satellites is transmitted to ground stations on Earth, where scientists use computers to help them interpret the satellite data. This technique is called image processing. It allows scientists to build up detailed maps of Earth that reveal features of our world that cannot be seen with the human eye alone.

Just like an image on a computer screen, a satellite image is made up of a number of picture elements, called **pixels**. Each pixel is like a single piece of information transmitted to Earth by the satellite. Putting all the pixels together builds up the picture.

This is a false-color image of Australia's Lake Carnegie, taken by Landsat 7. The image you see was put together from a *sensor* that used several different wavelengths to capture the lake in a unique way.

False colors

Plants reflect a lot of infrared light (see box), and a healthy plant reflects more than an unhealthy one. Infrared detectors in satellites can therefore monitor the health of the plants on Earth.

We cannot see infrared, so we use computers to make the images visible to us. Computers are used to give every pixel a brightness value, resulting in a gray scale, or black-and-white image. Human eyes are not very good at distinguishing shades of gray—after about 16 we cannot see the differences anymore. A computer, on the other hand, can tell thousands of gray shades apart. The researcher can use the computer to apply "false colors" to make things easier to see—for example, using red to show the infrared light reflected from plants.

A Landsat 7 image of Phoenix, Arizona, without the addition of false colors.

Another Landsat 7 image of Phoenix. This image has been enhanced with false colors.

Pseudo-color

A pseudo-color image is one in which a particular feature can be highlighted by color coding. The colors used can be completely different from the "true" colors. For example, some satellites use radar to measure the heights of mountains and other features. By giving different colors to different heights on the landscape, we can tell at once where the high and low areas are just by looking at the image. Another use would be to highlight temperature differences, such as showing warm and cold areas in the ocean.

THE ELECTROMAGNETIC SPECTRUM

The electromagnetic spectrum is the name for a range of different types of energy that travel through space in the form of waves. Some of these waves, called light waves, are visible to us.

The longest waves are radio waves. This is the energy that carries the music you listen to on the radio. Next come microwaves, followed by infrared. The warmth you feel from the Sun comes from infrared **radiation**. Next is visible light, which we detect with our eyes. Ultraviolet light is invisible to us, but some insects can detect it. It is ultraviolet radiation from the Sun that causes sunburn. Luckily for us, most of the harmful ultraviolet radiation is blocked by the **ozone** layer in the atmosphere. Beyond ultraviolet are the high-energy X-rays and gamma rays.

All of these forms of radiation are given off by various objects in space. Astronomers use them to build up a picture of the universe that is richer than would be possible with our eyes alone.

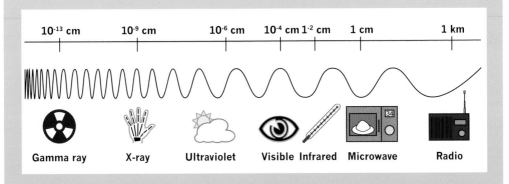

| 10^{-13} cm | 10^{-9} cm | 10^{-6} cm | 10^{-4} cm 1^{-2} cm | 1 cm | 1 km |

Gamma ray   X-ray   Ultraviolet   Visible Infrared Microwave   Radio

THE ACTIVE EARTH

Every so often an enormous earthquake or volcanic eruption occurs somewhere in the world. What causes these natural disasters?

The seemingly solid surface of Earth is broken up into a number of huge sections called **plates**. These are around 100 kilometers (62 miles) thick. They are made up of Earth's crust (the rocky outer skin of the planet) and part of the **mantle** (a semisolid layer that lies beneath the crust). Slow currents rising up from the hot interior of Earth carry the plates around like luggage on a slow-moving airport conveyor belt.

The study of these plate movements is called plate tectonics. Where the plates meet and collide with each other is where earthquakes and volcanoes happen. Over millions of years, the slow movements of the plates can push up mountain ranges and open up oceans.

Scientists use **satellite** observations to monitor these movements, giving early warnings of events such as volcanic eruptions and helping to guide emergency services to the right places.

This photo shows the Soufrière Hills volcano on the Caribbean island of Montserrat. This photo was taken with a digital camera by an astronaut aboard the International Space Station.

Watching the world move

Careful measurements of the seabed made from ships provided the first evidence to support the idea that Earth's surface is made up of moving plates. Today, observations from satellites using technology such as the Global Positioning System (GPS; see pages 44–45) has made monitoring these slow changes in Earth's surface easier to track. The highly detailed information obtained from satellites has provided proof that Earth's surface does indeed shift.

Earthquake prediction

Earthquakes are the result of huge energies building up, perhaps over the course of years. These energies form deep inside Earth as two plates move slowly alongside each other. Where the plates meet is called a fault line. If we had a way of detecting the buildup of energy, then steps could be taken to get people to safety ahead of the quake.

Satellite technology could have the answer. One possibility is called InSAR. This involves using **radar** images of an area to detect movements of the ground that are as slow as 1 millimeter a year. With these images, scientists can watch fault lines carefully to spot where stresses are building up.

A NEW OCEAN?

A new body of water may one day flood into one of the world's driest places. In the deserts of Ethiopia, in Africa, two of Earth's plates are slowly moving apart. Satellite images have shown a huge tear opening up. One day, water may rush in from the Red Sea to begin the formation of a new ocean. But it is a slow process. The plates are only moving about as fast as your fingernails grow.

Scientists think this Ethiopian desert on its way to becoming a new ocean

WORD STORE   **orbit** path followed by a smaller object around a larger one in space

Early warning

In 2004 thousands of people lost their lives around the coasts of South Asia when their communities were devastated by a massive **tsunami**. The cause of the tsunami was an earthquake under the ocean that lifted up the seabed, setting the wave in motion. The tsunami raced across 1,800 kilometers (1,118 miles) of ocean in just two hours. Earthquake scientists recorded the earthquake, but could not alert people quickly enough to help them escape the tsunami.

The Indonesian island of Sumatra, before (left) and after (right) the tsunami struck.

DART

In 2001 the first six Deep-Ocean Assessment and Reporting of Tsunamis (DART) systems were put in place in the Pacific Ocean. Ocean-floor **sensors** detect earthquakes and send signals to buoys floating on the ocean surface. These in turn signal satellites **orbiting** overhead.

Scientists monitoring the satellites will know almost at once if there is danger of a tsunami. They can figure out where, and how hard, it will hit, and send that information as quickly as possible to the endangered areas. After the 2004 disaster, scientists and politicians worked to set up a tsunami early warning system in the Indian Ocean as well.

WORD STORE   **tsunami** fast-moving wave triggered by an earthquake beneath the ocean

Volcano monitoring

Researchers have developed a variety of ways to monitor volcanoes for signs that an eruption may be about to happen. Satellite observations can detect some of the changes that warn of an eruption.

Scientists can track changes in temperature by looking at **infrared** images of volcanoes taken by satellites. Heat maps of the volcano pick out hot spots where hot **magma** (melted rock inside Earth's crust) is rising to the surface—a sign that an eruption might be about to take place. In 1998 satellite infrared detectors warned that Pacya, in Guatemala, was going to erupt a week before it happened.

InSAR radar mapping (see page 28) can be used to monitor volcanoes, too. Because of pressures inside, volcanoes are always changing shape. But these changes may be too small or over too wide an area to be seen easily from the ground.

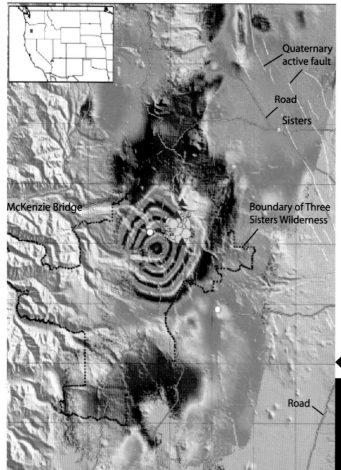

Quaternary active fault

Road

Sisters

McKenzie Bridge

Boundary of Three Sisters Wilderness

Road

In 2001 scientists were examining InSAR images of the area to the west of South Sister volcano, in the Three Sisters region of the central Oregon Cascade Range. They spotted a swelling in the ground. The swelling covered an area 15 to 20 kilometers (9 to 12 miles) across, and the maximum rise at its center was about 10 centimeters (4 inches). This was too broad and low to be noticed from the ground.

◄ ■■■■■■■■■■■■■■■■■■■■

This InSAR image from NASA shows the swelling in the ground near South Sister volcano.

WORD STORE   **infrared** type of radiation that lies beyond red in the electromagnetic spectrum

In 2004 a series of hundreds of minor earthquakes struck around the raised area. At present, the swelling of the ground appears to have lessened, but scientists are still keeping a careful watch on the area.

After the eruption

No amount of monitoring can prevent an eruption from taking place, but satellites still have a helpful role to play. When the Soufrière Hills volcano on Montserrat Island, in the Caribbean, erupted on May 20, 2006, about 90 million cubic meters (over 3 billion cubic feet) of material exploded out. A cloud of ash and volcanic gas over 17 kilometers (11 miles) high boiled up into the atmosphere. (See photo on page 27.)

As EOS's Aqua satellite passed over the region, it was able to follow the movement of the cloud. About one day after the eruption, Aqua showed the cloud south of Puerto Rico. By the next day it was south of Jamaica, about 1,600 kilometers (994 miles) west of Montserrat Island. Aqua's tracking allowed airliners to be directed safely around the cloud as it moved across the Caribbean.

The MODIS instrument aboard Terra captured this image of the ash cloud erupting from the Soufrière Hills volcano. The volcano is in the upper right corner of the image.

WORD STORE　　　**magma**　melted rock inside Earth's crust

THE LIVING PLANET

Earth is a living world. Life is found across its land surfaces and in its oceans. In addition to keeping an eye on the planet itself, **satellites** can also keep a watch on the living things that make their homes there. Satellites can be used to give our planet a regular checkup by monitoring patterns of vegetation on land, changes in the oceans, and the quality of the air. A healthy living planet Earth is good for humanity's health, too.

In December 1968 the Apollo 8 astronauts became the first humans to **orbit** the Moon. It was the first time humans had seen our home from deep space. The photographs they took of Earth in space changed the way we thought about our planet.

Earth-observation satellites let us track animals in a way that researchers on the ground, or in the ocean, could never hope to do. Mapping animals' movements from space has opened up a whole new world of understanding about Earth's wildlife.

Marine monitoring

Satellite tracking of wildlife can be of great help in understanding animals that are hard to watch directly. It is also extremely valuable for scientists trying to keep an eye on endangered species.

Satellite tracking lets scientists monitor ocean-living animals like whales, sharks, and tuna that would otherwise be impossible to follow. Two types of tags are used. A pop-up tag stores all the information it collects and then transmits it to the satellite in a single burst when its battery dies. The other type collects data while the animal is underwater, and then transmits it to the satellite when the animal surfaces.

These tags are small enough to fit in the palm of your hand. Information gathered includes the animal's location, how deep it dives, how long it dives for, and how much time it spends on the surface. Satellite tags can last from a few days to many months, depending on battery life.

Follow that bear!

Polar bears are big, powerful animals, but they are vulnerable to changes in their **environment**. **Climate change** could mean that there will be less sea ice in the Arctic where the bears live. The bears use the sea ice as platforms to hunt from. If the ice melts early, the bears get less to eat. This means they have less body fat to keep them warm when winter returns.

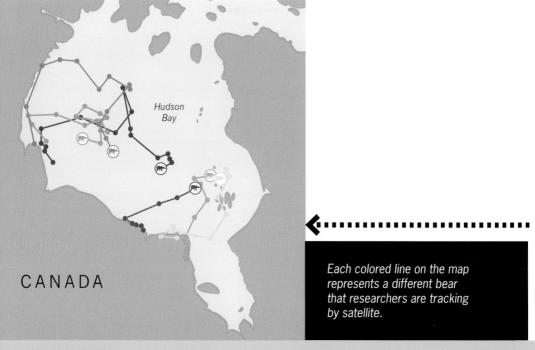

Hudson Bay

CANADA

Each colored line on the map represents a different bear that researchers are tracking by satellite.

WORD STORE   **tranquilizer** substance that puts an animal to sleep temporarily so it can be handled safely

Norwegian scientists tracked one bear swimming at least 74 kilometers (46 miles) in a single day. "This time we have data showing how long the bear was in the water," said Jon Aars, a researcher at the Norwegian Polar Institute. "This is an astonishing swim."

Another scientist used satellite tracking to follow a female bear as she traveled on a 4,800-kilometer (3,000-mile) journey across the Arctic. That's about the same distance as 115 marathons!

A scientist attaches a satellite tracking collar to a tranquilized polar bear in Canada.

With the help of satellite technology, scientists can follow the wanderings of polar bears from space to see where they go to feed and to have their cubs. A bear is tracked by helicopter and knocked out with **tranquilizer** darts, which make it sleep. While the bear sleeps, scientists check its health and fit it with a radio collar. The scientists make sure they are a safe distance away when the bear wakes up again! Only female polar bears can be tracked using radio collars. A male polar bear's neck is wider than its head, so the collars just slide off.

SeaStar

In addition to watching the animals that live in the world's oceans, satellites are also watching the oceans themselves.

SeaWiFS is the Sea-Viewing Wide Field-of-View **Sensor** carried aboard the SeaStar satellite (also known as OrbView-2). It is used to monitor Earth's oceans, keeping track of how clear the water is and checking on concentrations of **phytoplankton**.

SeaStar was sent into orbit in an unusual way, Rather than using a big rocket **launcher**, the satellite was mounted on the smaller Pegasus launch vehicle. This was carried up very high in the air by a specially modified aircraft before being fired into orbit.

Scientist James Yoder watched the launch on the monitors at Vandenberg Air Force Base. He said, "I waited for a final countdown to launch and was startled to see the Pegasus drop suddenly and unannounced (at least to me) from the plane. Pegasus fell for what seemed to be a very long time (actually only five seconds) until finally the main engine lit up."

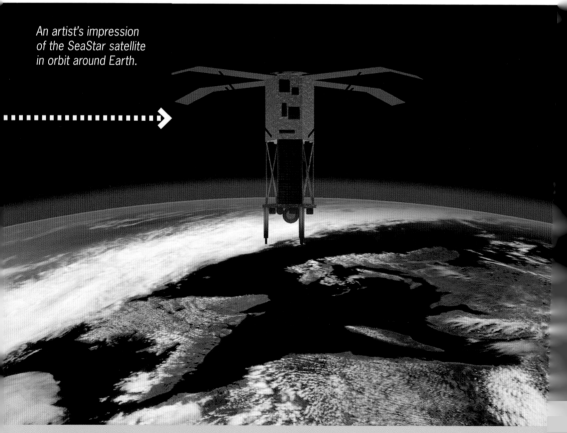

An artist's impression of the SeaStar satellite in orbit around Earth.

WORD STORE   **altimeter** instrument used to measure height above ground, or altitude

Jason-2

The Ocean Surface Topography Mission (OSTM)/Jason-2 is an international mission developed jointly by NASA and the French space agency CNES. CNES provided the spacecraft, and NASA and CNES jointly provided the instruments that are carried on board. NASA was responsible for launching the Delta II rocket that carried it into orbit.

Jason-2 was launched on June 20, 2008, from Vandenberg Air Force Base. It is in a 1,336-kilometer (830-mile) circular orbit tilted at an angle to Earth's equator. This allows it to monitor 95 percent of Earth's oceans every 10 days.

The main instrument on board Jason-2 is an **altimeter**. This highly accurate instrument can measure the distance between the satellite and the ocean surface to within a few centimeters. Jason-2 closely monitors sea levels, allowing scientists to keep a close eye on any changes. Rising sea levels are one of the most important effects of climate change.

Jason-2 works together with the earlier Jason-1 satellite to provide very detailed measurements. These measurements can be used to calculate the speed and direction of ocean currents, temperature changes in the oceans, and levels in rivers and lakes. This information is useful for such things as planning the best routes for shipping, monitoring fish stocks, and long-range weather forecasting.

This map from Jason-2 provides scientists with details on wave heights in the world's oceans.

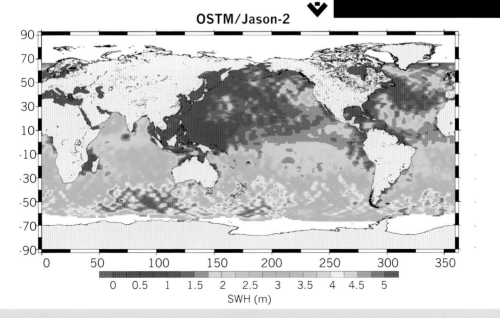

OSTM/Jason-2

SWH (m)

The world and its weather

Weather watching is one of the most important things that satellites do—ever since the first weather satellite, Vanguard 2, was launched on February 17, 1959.

Weather satellites are either placed in polar orbits, where they monitor the whole planet over a period of time, or into geostationary orbit, where they always watch the same area.

Nimbus

The Nimbus satellites were some of the earliest and most important weather watchers. Seven were launched over 14 years, beginning with Nimbus 1 in August 1964. Lessons learned from Nimbus were very important in designing the Earth-observation satellites that followed. Nimbus technology led directly to the instruments carried on board Terra and Aqua (see pages 14 to 19).

Before Nimbus, the idea that a satellite far above the planet could measure air temperature and pressure, water vapor in clouds, and ocean temperatures, seemed far-fetched. Nimbus made it a reality. For the first time, weather forecasts that were accurate over several days became possible.

Guided by Nimbus

Nimbus also pioneered ground-to-satellite-to-ground communications, technology that would be essential in developing global satellite positioning (GPS; see pages 44 and 45). Ground-based weather stations in remote areas could transmit information to the Nimbus satellites, which would relay it to researchers elsewhere.

This image from Terra shows a hurricane in the Atlantic. Without Nimbus, we wouldn't have Terra!

THE SOIL MOISTURE AND OCEAN SALINITY PROJECT

The water cycle is one of the most important factors influencing Earth's climate. Ocean currents carry warm and cold water around the world. The movements of these currents are affected by the amount of salt in the water.

Measuring the salt in the oceans was a difficult task. The European Space Agency's SMOS (Soil, Moisture, and Ocean Salinity) Project took 10 years developing a new instrument called MIRAS. Its job is to detect moisture in soil and salt content in water.

Liquid water and dry soil compared to pure water and saltwater give off different amounts of energy. MIRAS has microwave sensors that can detect these differences. Ordinarily this would have needed a very big antenna, which would have been difficult to get into orbit. So, instead MIRAS has three arms covered with a total of 69 small antennae. These little antennae work together like one big one and can detect 0.1 gram (0.004 ounce) of salt in 1 liter of seawater. The data from MIRAS is another step toward accurate weather predictions.

The SMOS satellite in orbit.

The Defense Meteorological Satellite Program

The Defense Meteorological Satellite Program (DMSP) was originally a secret program run by the U.S. Air Force. Program 35, as it was originally called, was intended to help military planners by giving them accurate information about weather conditions. This would help, for example, when spy-plane missions needed to be planned. Today, the U.S. Air Force Space and Missile Systems Center at Los Angeles Air Force Base is responsible for maintaining the DMSP satellites.

The DMSP has been in operation for five decades, and aging satellites are periodically replaced. DMSP 15, the most recent, was launched on December 12, 1999. The satellites are placed in sun-synchronous orbits. Some observe the nighttime Earth, some observe daytime, and others are positioned to watch the surface at dawn and dusk. Each satellite sees the whole planet twice a day.

NOAA

The DMSP data are sent to the NOAA's (National Oceanic and Atmospheric Administration's) Earth Observation Group, which maintains an archive (collection) of this valuable weather information. Everyday data from four DMSP satellites are added to the archive.

NOAA weather maps like this one rely on information from satellites.

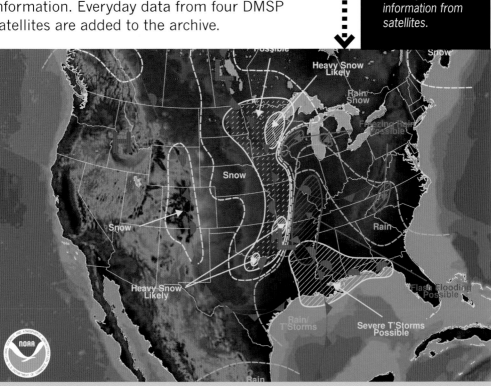

This DMSP satellite image is from 1979. It shows monsoon effects over India.

NOAA scientists monitor conditions in the world's oceans and atmosphere, carry out research into the ocean environment and climate change, and warn of weather hazards. NOAA also operates its own Geostationary Operational Environmental Satellites (GOES). GOES orbit 35,800 kilometers (22,300 miles) above Earth's equator, maintaining position over the same part of the surface.

GOES-East and GOES-West cover Alaska, Hawaii, the entire continental United States, and the Pacific and Atlantic oceans. The satellites take photographs every 15 minutes, keeping a watch for severe weather conditions such as snowstorms and hurricanes. If you are watching a television weather report in the United States, the pictures you see on the screen will have come from one of those two satellites.

Sensors on board GOES also detect cloud, land, and ocean temperatures and monitor solar activity. GOES 15 is due to be launched in March 2010.

GOES TO THE RESCUE

In addition to their weather-watching activities, NOAA's GOES provide another valuable service. They are used to detect when satellite emergency locator beacons have been activated, helping search-and-rescue teams to reach people in danger as quickly as possible.

PEOPLE
AND
PLANET

Earth is our home. People and their activities have transformed the surface of Earth and the air that surrounds it. Earth-observation **satellites** can help us keep watch on these changes. Using the information sent down from space, we can map levels of pollution over cities and see how the wind carries that pollution across borders from one country to another.

Satellites in space have transformed the way we live. Communications satellites make it possible for a person anywhere in the world to talk to another person anywhere else. From space, satellites can monitor the growth of our cities. They can see how much land is being farmed—and how much forest has been cut down to make way for that farmland. They can keep track of shipping, and tell us, via GPS (the Global Positioning System), how to get to where we want to go.

This image is constructed from DMSP data. It shows the lights of Earth's cities at night.

Reference points in space

Out in space at a distance of over 19,000 kilometers (11,800 miles), a constellation of 24 solar-powered (Sun-powered) satellites circles Earth. These satellites are the Global Positioning System, or GPS, operated by the U.S. Air Force. Each one has been placed into a precise **orbit**. Ground-based **radar** systems track the satellites with great accuracy, monitoring the slightest variation in their orbits. Their exact positions are known moment to moment.

Russia is putting its own system in place called the Global Navigation Satellite System (Glonass). Eighteen satellites covering the entire territory of the Russian Federation are currently in orbit. Another six satellites will have to be launched to provide services worldwide. A European project called Galileo hopes to have 30 GPS satellites in orbit by 2013.

Where in the world am I?

Each GPS satellite transmits a constant signal, which can be picked up by a GPS receiver. Because the satellites are all at different distances, the signals reach the receiver at slightly different times. The receiver accurately calculates its distance from each of four different satellites based on the time it takes for the signals to arrive. It then uses that information to figure out your position on the surface of Earth.

Considering the distances involved to the GPS satellites, the position determined by GPS is very accurate. Your position on Earth can be placed to within about 10 meters (33 feet) using a handheld GPS receiver.

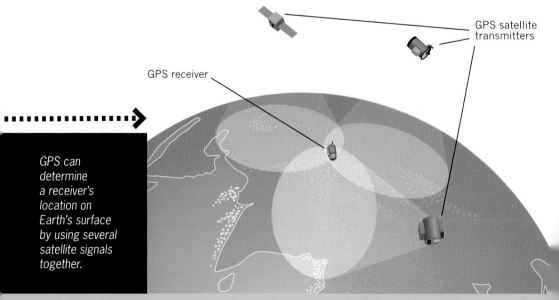

GPS satellite transmitters

GPS receiver

GPS can determine a receiver's location on Earth's surface by using several satellite signals together.

WORD STORE   **surveyor** person who measures the distance of things for maps

The uses of GPS

Hikers can use handheld GPS receivers to help navigate their way across tricky terrain. GPS receivers can be especially useful if the weather turns bad and map reading becomes difficult. A vehicle-mounted GPS can display a road map for drivers and tell them the best route to take to go from one place to another. Police and rescue services can use GPS to determine the nearest vehicles to an emergency, so they can get to where they need to be as swiftly as possible.

GPS is one of the ways by which we really do map Earth from space. **Surveyors** and mapmakers use GPS to calculate positions that might have taken days to do using other methods.

This hiker is using a map and a handheld GPS receiver to keep from getting lost.

GPS preserves the rain forest

GPS is also being used to protect the rain forests of South America. The native peoples of the Amazon are using GPS and other modern technologies alongside their traditional knowledge to conserve the forests.

The Amazon Conservation Team (ACT) works with South American governments and 32 tribes of indigenous (native) peoples in the use of GPS and the Internet to map, manage, and protect the rain forests. ACT partners closely with Chief Almir and the Surui tribe in the southwest Amazon. Before getting involved with ACT, Chief Almir traveled to the United States in 2007 to meet the people at Google Earth (a project that allows anyone with Internet access to view detailed images of Earth). "He asked us to train his people so they could tell their story, their history, and the beauty of their land and culture and gain support from the world to fight the loss of the forest," said one of the people he met. ACT supplied the Surui with laptops, GPS, and other gadgets.

Pinpointing the damage

A great deal of damage is done to the rain forests by illegal miners looking for gold. Because this area is so remote (far-off), mining operations can be difficult to detect. Now the Surui can use the Internet and Google Earth at ACT offices to check for signs of miners. The high-resolution satellite imagery makes these things much easier to see.

Before GPS was available, a Surui might come upon a mining operation on the ground but would have no map on which to mark its position. Now he can pinpoint the location using GPS.

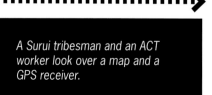

A Surui tribesman and an ACT worker look over a map and a GPS receiver.

From MODIS aboard Terra, this image shows a section of the Amazon in Brazil. Deforested areas appear tan and pale green. The Brazilian government uses images like this to detect illegal logging.

Satellites and rain forests

It is not just important to preserve the rain forests for the good of the people who live there. Looking after the rain forest is also a way of helping to fight global warming and **climate change**. Plants take in carbon dioxide (one of the **greenhouse gases** responsible for global warming) when they grow, and they release it when they are burned or left to rot. The destruction of forests across Earth is estimated to release one-fifth of the greenhouse gases that are due to human activity.

Space agencies like NASA and the European Space Agency are involved in an international project to monitor the world's forests from space. Satellite images from Landsat dating back to 1972 can let us see how much of the world's forests have been lost since then. Under the new project, satellite mapping will first measure the size of a country's forests. In a second phase, radar images will be used to measure how much carbon is locked up in each forest. The plan is to slow the loss of forests by giving nations "carbon credits" based on the size of their forests.

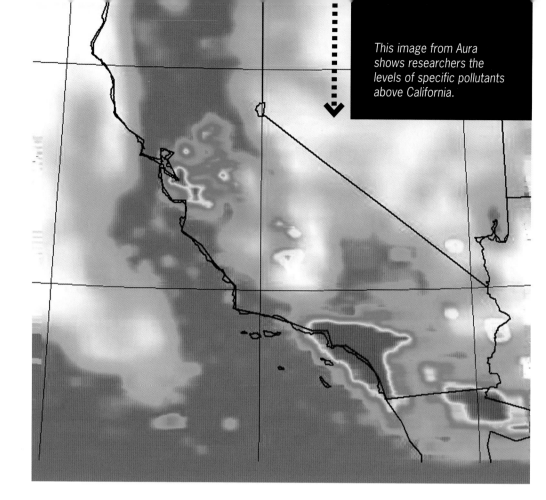

This image from Aura shows researchers the levels of specific pollutants above California.

Aura

Satellite instruments that can detect harmful chemicals such as nitrogen dioxide and **ozone** in the atmosphere allow scientists to monitor sources of air pollution. One of the satellites involved in this pollution watch is Aura, another of the EOS family of satellites.

Aura is the last of the A-Train satellites, following about seven minutes behind Aqua, CloudSat, and CALIPSO (see pages 18 and 19). It was launched into a near-polar, sun-synchronous orbit on July 15, 2004, and takes 100 minutes to orbit Earth. Over a 16-day period it passes over almost every point on Earth's surface.

Aura carries a sophisticated package of instruments that monitor the ozone layer and levels of **pollutants** in the atmosphere. When the Chinese authorities banned cars from Beijing before the 2008 Olympic Games, Aura detected a 50 percent drop in levels of nitrogen dioxide around the city.

WORD STORE   **aerosol** cloud of particles suspended in a gas

Future missions

Earth-science space missions are planned for launch up to 2017, and probably beyond.

Aquarius, scheduled for launch in May 2010, will measure the saltiness of the oceans, the first NASA mission to do so. Principal investigator Gary Lagerloef has been working on the project since 2003. He is eager for his work to benefit the public, not just scientists, saying, "We live on this planet. All of us feel that we want our work to have relevance to the public and not just let it collect dust somewhere in a scientific journal."

The Glory mission is due to be launched into low Earth orbit around October 2010. The mission will be part of the U.S. Climate Change Science Program (CCSP).

Glory will collect data on **aerosols** in the atmosphere, including soot from burning fuels. It will also measure the amount of energy reaching Earth from the Sun. This data will help scientists to determine to what extent (if any) global warming can be explained by natural causes. Glory's information will be very important in predicting future climate change, and in helping us decide how best to respond to changes in our **environment**.

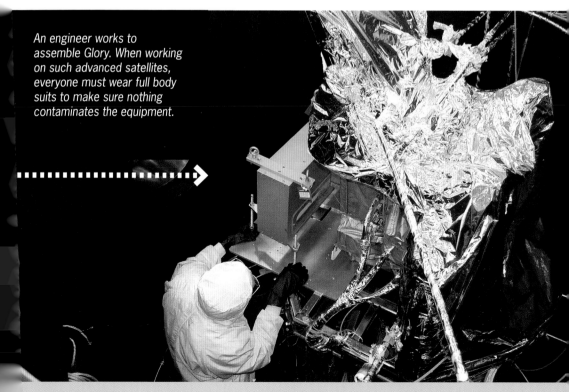

An engineer works to assemble Glory. When working on such advanced satellites, everyone must wear full body suits to make sure nothing contaminates the equipment.

WORD STORE   **pollutant** unwanted chemical found in the environment that came as the result of human activities

TIMELINE OF MAPPING EARTH

October 4, 1957 Sputnik 1, the world's first artificial satellite, is launched.

February 1, 1958 Explorer 1 is launched. It helps scientists discover that Earth is surrounded by bands of radiation.

March 17, 1958 Vanguard 1 is launched. Today, it is the oldest satellite still in orbit.

April 1, 1960 Tiros 1, the first television weather satellite, is launched.

August 12, 1960 Echo 1, the first communications satellite, is launched.

April 12, 1961 Yuri Gagarin becomes the first person to orbit Earth.

July 10, 1962 Telstar relays the first transatlantic (crossing the Atlantic) television programs.

August 19, 1964 Syncom, the first communications satellite to be placed in a geostationary orbit, is launched.

February 3, 1966 Luna 9 becomes the first spacecraft to land on the Moon.

▼

December 24, 1968 The crew of Apollo 8 become the first people to orbit the Moon and the first to see Earth from deep space.

▼

July 20, 1969 The crew of Apollo 11 become the first people to land on the surface of the Moon.

▼

July 23, 1972 Landsat 1, the first satellite to monitor Earth's resources, is launched.

▼

April 12, 1981 The first space shuttle mission is launched.

▼

April, 1995 The Global Positioning System becomes fully operational.

▼

December 18, 1999 Terra, the Earth Observing System's flagship satellite, is launched.

▼

October 31, 2000 The first crew arrives at the International Space Station.

▼

May 2, 2002 Aqua, the leading satellite of the A-Train, is launched.

▼

February 24, 2009 The Orbiting Carbon Observatory is lost when it fails to reach orbit.

GLOSSARY

aerosol a cloud of tiny solid or liquid particles that are suspended in a gas. Smoke is a type of aerosol.

altimeter an instrument that is used to measure the height above ground, or altitude

climate change usually this refers to the changes in the Earth's climate that many scientists believe are being caused as a result of human activities

energy balance the Earth's energy balance is the balance between the energy coming in from the Sun and the energy reflected back out into space as heat. Changes in the energy balance result in changes in the climate.

environment the world's living things and the places in which they make their homes

greenhouse gas a gas in the atmosphere that absorbs heat and reflects it back to the Earth rather than letting it escape into space and therefore upset the Earth's energy balance

infrared a type of radiation that lies beyond red in the electromagnetic spectrum; infrared is sometimes also known as heat rays

launcher the vehicle that carries a satellite up into orbit

legend a list that explains the different symbols used on a map

magma melted rock inside the Earth's crust; when magma reaches the surface it is called lava

mantle the layer inside the Earth that lies between the crust and the core

orbit the path followed by a smaller object around a larger one in space; satellites orbit the Earth and the Earth orbits the Sun, for example

ozone a type of oxygen found high in the atmosphere that filters out much of the harmful ultraviolet radiation from the Sun; ozone at ground level is actually a harmful pollutant

payload the cargo transported by a rocket launcher into orbit; this could be a satellite or a crewed capsule

payload bay the space shuttle's cargo hold, used to transport satellites and other equipment into orbit

phytoplankton microscopic living things that live in water and can make their own food by capturing energy from the Sun

pixel the smallest item of information in an image; one of the tiny dots that together form a picture on a computer or television screen

plate rigid section of the Earth's crust that is continually moving at a rate of a few centimeters a year

pollutant unwanted, often harmful, chemical found in the environment as a result of human activities

radar a measuring instrument that determines the distance to an object by bouncing waves off of it

radiation energy that travels in the form of waves

satellite a device placed in orbit, usually around the Earth or Moon. Satellites are often used for collecting information and for communication.

sensor a device that detects something, such as a change in light levels or the amount of a chemical present

surveyor a person who accurately measures positions and distances of objects on the ground so they can be plotted on a map

tranquilizer a substance that is used to put animals to sleep temporarily so they can be handled safely

tsunami a fast-moving wave that is triggered by an earthquake beneath the ocean

ultraviolet a type of radiation that lies beyond violet in the electromagnetic spectrum; ultraviolet rays from the Sun cause sunburn

FIND OUT MORE

BOOKS

Angelo, Joseph A. *Satellites (Frontiers in Space)*. New York: Facts on File, 2006.

Asimov, Isaac and Richard Hantula. *The Earth*. Amherst, NY: Prometheus Books, 2004.

Miller, Ron. *Satellites (Space Innovations)*. Minneapolis, MN: Twenty First Century Books, 2007.

Rudy, Lisa Jo. *Eyes in the Sky*. New York: Children's Press, 2007.

Zuehlke, Jeffrey. *Earth (Early Bird Astronomy)*. Minneapolis, MN: Lerner Publications, 2009.

WEBSITES

Google Earth
http://earth.google.com/

Studying the Earth from Space
http://nasascience.nasa.gov/earth-science

The Aqua Mission
http://nasascience.nasa.gov/missions/aqua

The Terra Mission
http://nasascience.nasa.gov/missions/terra

The National Oceanic and Atmospheric Administration
http://www.noaa.gov

Types of Orbit
http://marine.rutgers.edu/mrs/education/class/paul/orbits2.html

Track the Positions of Satellites in Space.
http://science.nasa.gov/realtime/jtrack/3d/JTrack3D.html

Global Positioning Satellites
http://www.nasm.si.edu/gps/

Using Satellites to Help with Conservation
http://e360.yale.edu/content/feature.msp?id=2134

Satellite Images of Environmental Change
http://earthshots.usgs.gov/tableofcontents

Earth Now! Landsat Image Viewer
http://earthnow.usgs.gov

Our Earth as Art
http://earhtasart.gsfc.nasa.gov/index.htm

PLACES TO VISIT

Smithsonian National Air and Space Museum
National Mall Building
6th and Independence Avenue
Washington, DC 20560

http://www.nasm.si.edu/

Goddard Space Flight Center
8800 Greenbelt Road
Greenbelt, MD 20771

http://www.nasa.gov/centers/goddard/home/index.html

Jet Propulsion Laboratory
4800 Oak Grove Drive
Pasadena
CA 91109-8099

http://www.jpl.nasa.gov/events/tours.cfm

See a rocket launch.
Check here for a list of NASA's upcoming launches and
information about the best places to see a rocket take off
for space.

http://www.nasa.gov/missions/highlights/schedule.html

INDEX

**Indianapolis
Marion County
Public Library**

**Renew by Phone
269-5222**

**Renew on the Web
www.imcpl.org**

For General Library Information
please call 269-1700

DEMCO